The Answer

Putting an End to the Search for Life Satisfaction

Randy Pope

LIFE-ON-LIFE RESOURCES
a division of Life-on-Life Ministries

The Answer
2nd Printing (Revised)

Copyright © 2005, © 2007

Life-on-Life Resources
A Division of Life-on-Life Ministries
9500 Medlock Bridge Road
Duluth, Ga 30097

ISBN 13-digit: 978-0-9776605-0-6
ISBN 10-digit: 0-9776605-0-8

Cover Design: Zoe Hammond Huff

Cover Photo: Adobe Systems Incorporated

Printing: Canterbury Press

Printed in the United States of America

Library of Congress Control Number: 2005937543

I dedicate this book to Jim Baird and Frank Barker,
who marked my life in such a significant manner
that I can experience daily what I write in this book.

TABLE OF CONTENTS

INTRODUCTION

◆ What every young person should learn.

◆ What every suicide victim should have known.

◆ What every depressed person should realize.

◆ What every religious moralist, irreligious immoralist and Christian should understand.

I have a passion. I love to have lunch with people to talk about their spiritual pilgrimage. After meeting with hundreds of moral and immoral, religious and irreligious people, I am convinced of this—all are looking for the same thing. It's as if all are in a race to put a puzzle together which, when completed, will give meaning to life.

But there is an insurmountable problem. A major piece is missing. In fact, of all the pieces, if this piece is missing the puzzle can never make sense. And time and time again, I watch lives take on unparalleled meaning and satisfaction when this piece of the puzzle is found and put in place.

No, it's not praying a prayer to become a Christian. Many a true believer today is living a meaningless and unsatisfying life. Neither is the answer found in the commonly encouraged foundational disciplines of Christian living.

So the critical question is, "What is this piece and where is it found?" This book answers this question; thus the title, The Answer. The first of three segments will identify the missing piece and the next two will show us how to find it.

Because this answer has to do with a rarely understood biblical teaching, many longtime, well-studied Christians tell me that this piece has radically changed their lives. They say it becomes a lens through which they now see all of life differently. This was certainly the case for me.

If this critical piece to life's puzzle is missing in your life, I hope you will find it and have a life full of meaning and satisfaction. This is my prayer for you as you begin reading.

DESPERATE TO UNDERSTAND
THREE WORDS

"I'M PLANNING TO end my life. It will happen in a few days—at the end of the Christmas holidays. Only you will know that it wasn't an accident. Frankly, I'm looking forward to dying. I have no reason to continue living."

I saw her expression. This was no "wolf cry" for attention. It was a last-ditch effort to see if there was some purpose for living that she had missed in her nearly 50 years of walking this planet.

Since I had never met this woman, I was curious. "What caused you to come talk with me?"

She explained that over the past year, her son and his wife had been attending our church. During that time they had experienced a radical life change. Though she held little hope for finding meaning from religion, she realized there was nothing to lose in meeting with me.

What a contrast of emotions I experienced as I listened to her story. On the one hand, I hurt for her in her deep sense of hopelessness. Yet on the other hand, I could hardly contain my eagerness to introduce her to three words that I was confident would end her lifelong search.

After hearing the final details of her disappointing life and her many dead-end searches for something that could make her life meaningful, I surprised her with what I said. "Judy, I have to commend you. You are smarter than most of us. You have discovered something that many never realize. You've realized that there is nothing in this world that can give your life meaning. You have come, in a sense, to the end of life's internet, while the rest of us are surfing away with the hope of finding what you

"You have come to the end of life's internet."

know isn't there. You know that when hope is gone, the desire to live is gone too."

As you would assume, I needed to say more than simply commending her insight about life's hopelessness. I vividly remember the thrill I experienced when I introduced her to three words that unlock the meaning to life. I couldn't help but anticipate her eyes brightening as I explained these words.

The reason for my anticipation was based on untold numbers of weekly conversations like this with depressed students, religious and irreligious people, moral and immoral businessmen, professional athletes, discouraged divorcees . . . the list could go on and on. Repeatedly, I hear the same response—that these three words, when their meanings are unpacked, explain a lifelong search for satisfaction. The three words are "glory," "grace," and "truth."

I introduced the first of these words to Judy. "Glory" would best be understood in the context of a story.

PART ONE

The Story of Glory

INTRODUCTION TO "THE STORY OF GLORY"

Whether helping Judy, who was contemplating suicide, or talking to John, whom I met for lunch after being introduced at a golf outing, or meeting Charles, who was disillusioned with life as a college student, it's not long before I ask, "Have you ever heard 'The Story of Glory'?" Of course, I already know their answer.

Not only have they not heard this story, but I would be amazed if they knew the meaning of glory as it is used in the Bible. By the way, do you know what a concordance is? It's a reference tool used to locate any word in the Bible. Try looking up "glory" sometime and see what you find. It's used over 300 times.

Most students of the Bible are familiar with the word "glory" when referring to either the glory *of* God or giving glory *to* God. But few have considered it in terms of the glory that comes *from* God. "The Story of Glory" is about this latter usage. It describes the glory that comes from God and is given to people who are prepared to receive it.

The essence of glory is satisfaction.

But what exactly is "glory"? It is often defined as "renown, fame, honor, or beauty."[1] A more comprehensive definition describes it as "the condition of highest achievement, prosperity, pleasure, pride, honor, admiration, splendor, magnificence."[2] For me the word that best captures the essence of glory is "satisfaction."

The essence of glory is satisfaction.

We are all familiar with our day-to-day common usage of this word. When we think of glory, we immediately think of its most noted recipients. What would happen if a world-famous athlete was invited to a high school? Students would scream as he walked into the building and applaud energetically when introduced. Even those who have no appreciation for sports would stand in line in hopes of getting an autograph. This athlete receives glory wherever he goes. He lives with renown, fame, and honor—presumably all anyone needs to be satisfied.

With only this general idea of the meaning of "glory," allow me to tell "The Story of Glory." This story explains Judy's search, her hopelessness, and even her eagerness to die. It explains John's seasonal contentment with a life of abundance. It explains Charles' lethargic pursuit of a college degree while watching his dream for a satisfied life become dimmer by the day. "The Story of Glory" is best understood with a brief explanation of its components in the following chapters.

THE SEARCH FOR GLORY

JUDY WAS EAGERLY waiting as I began to tell the story. This is how it begins:

Designed for Glory

The Bible is the story of both God and man. Its earliest chapters tell us of man's original design. He was brought into existence experiencing complete satisfaction, honor, and renown. The only other living being, God Himself, saw him as perfect in His own sight. Simply put, man was designed with full glory. Thus, "Designed with Glory" is the title of the first chapter.

Were it not for their embrace of the Evil One's luring temptation, our original forefather and mother—and all mankind living in their likeness—would be enjoying the fullness of glory. Life would be totally satisfying, self-esteem would be unfractured, and hopelessness would be non-existent.

Fall from Glory

All of this changes when we come to the second chapter, entitled "Fall from Glory." Because man does take the tempter's lure, he is immediately stripped of his cherished glory. The Bible clearly describes this loss in Romans 3:23: "All have sinned and fall short of the glory of God."

Perhaps until now, we find this story somewhat theoretical. But with the introduction of the third chapter, all that changes. This next chapter, "Search for Glory," becomes painfully self-revealing.

Search for Glory

We are designed to experience and enjoy the fullness of glory, and once it is missing, a search begins. To be without glory is unnatural. Searching for missing glory is instinctive. Though we may not know that's what is missing, we do know that something essential for life is lost.

As Blaise Pascal puts it:

> *All men seek happiness. This is without exception. Whatever different means they employ, they all tend to this end . . . the will never takes the least step but to this object. This is the motive of every action, of every man, even of those who hang themselves.*[3]

I can certainly relate to this. In fact, at this point I need to make a confession. I am a recovering applause addict. For years, I have lived for the response of applause. However, I am somewhat comforted by one reality. As the saying goes, "misery loves company." And I'm in a large company of fellow addicts.

Guess who else is an addict? You! You may be a recovering addict, but you are nevertheless an addict. For that matter, everyone to one degree or another is an applause addict. We *must* have glory.

Have you ever wondered why we care so much about how we look? Or obsess over our golf scores? Or why we hurt so badly when publicly embarrassed? Or why we become so despondent when rejected by those who we truly care about?

It's because we lost something necessary to our satisfaction, and we cannot be satisfied until we find it again. No wonder the search is so important to us—and so consuming of our time, money, emotional energy, and relational collateral.

After our fall from glory, we see all of life from a temporal perspective and find all our hope for satisfaction in temporal things. We go from garbage heap to garbage heap, toy to toy, fix to fix, and relationship to relationship in search of glory.

What's so deceptive is that at first embrace, each object seems to deliver the satisfaction we seek. But the satisfaction is short lived, and soon the search resumes. We think, "If only I had athletic or career success, popularity, the right spouse, etc., I would be satisfied." Yet regardless of the desire, once we obtain it, we will soon feel empty again. Whether from material items of great value or human relationships of exceptional beauty, the high doesn't linger for long.

That explains pop music icon Madonna's disillusionment with fame and fortune. In her own words: "Take it from me. I went down the road to 'be all you can be, realize your dreams', and I'm telling you that fame and fortune are not what they are cracked up to be."

> *"Fame and fortune are not what they are cracked up to be."*

The objects we pursue are in truth nothing more than counterfeits of real glory. Counterfeit glory becomes a narcotic. The more we get, the more we need. The more we need, the more dissatisfied we become. And the more dissatisfied we become, the greater extremes we will pursue to continue our search.

You tell me. Who is typically more satisfied with what they have? Those with their essential needs met, or those with an abundance? If I've heard it once, I've heard it a hundred times—"I've got everything I could want, but something's missing."

The late Greek ship owner and financier Aristotle Onassis is reported to have said, "I've just been a machine for making money. I seem to have spent my life in a golden tunnel looking for the outlet that would lead to happiness. But the tunnel kept going on. After my death there will be nothing left."

That's why Judy was ahead of most people. She had already discovered that she could search for the rest of her life and never be satisfied.

You see, you and I were designed to be satisfied only with the glory provided by God. Any counterfeit is defined in the Bible as an idol.

An idol is anyone or anything apart from true glory that we consider necessary for life satisfaction.

Judy, John, and Charles were all unknowingly in a search for glory, but they were grasping at counterfeits. It's the same for everyone everywhere. Each idol we obtain eventually leads to disappointment. In the truest sense, God could say, "I told you so." His own word in the Psalms puts it this way: "The sorrows of those who run after another god [idol, counterfeit glory] shall multiply."[4]

But this is where the story takes a turn for the better. In fact, the story becomes so good that we call it "gospel," which means "good news." The fourth chapter of "The Story of Glory" is titled, "Discovery of Glory." This is when Judy's eyes began to brighten.

THE DISCOVERY OF GLORY

Judy sat listening intently as I turned to the second half of the story.

Discovery of Glory

The incarnation (Christ becoming man) is described in the first chapter of John's gospel. The first two verses read, "In the beginning was the Word, and the Word was with God and the Word was God. He was with God in the beginning."[5] "Word" describes the role Jesus would play in being the communication link between God the Father and mankind.

Imagine having lunch with someone you've never met. After an hour of looking, waving, and nodding at one another, you leave. A mutual friend aware of your luncheon asks if you got to know one another. When you say "No," he asks, "Why not?" You would say, "Because not a word was spoken!" Jesus is that all-important Word making it possible to know God.

The apostle John continues his description of Jesus in verse fourteen. "The Word became flesh and made His dwelling among us, and we have seen His *glory*, the

Incarnation –taking on the human nature and form by Jesus.

glory of the One and Only, who came from the Father."[6] John describes Jesus in the context of His glory.

But the apostle Paul takes this even further in his letter to the people of Colossae. In Colossians he says that when Christ dwells in a person's life, He is that person's hope for glory.[7]

"Christ in you" is a way of describing the end of the search, the discovery of glory. Our second word will give a better explanation of this indwelling of Christ, but understand for now that this is what the Bible refers to as coming into a personal, life-changing encounter with God. This is where friendship with God begins. That's when those in broken relationship with God, stripped of His glory, get an initial infusion of that glory.

This encounter explains countless numbers of people throughout history who declare their search for meaning in life to have ended. It's the picture of the prodigal being embraced by his father. It's the story of the religious moralist who finally recognizes that though she is no worse than the prodigal, she is indeed worse off due to her greater difficulty in seeing her need for forgiveness. How challenging it is for people to acknowledge their own goodness as their greatest offense to God. I'll explain this reality a bit later.

This life-changing encounter is what Jesus described as a second birth (John 3:7). I realize that the religious term "born again" has a nasty sound. Because so many radical, religious oddballs have hidden behind this term to defend obnoxious communication and behavior, most of us have a knee-jerk reaction to it. But it originated with Jesus; He used it to describe the encounter with Him that qualifies people to receive glory.

When discussing spiritual formation with new friends, I often draw three boxes. Each represents an option that best describes where they are in their spiritual pilgrimage.

I write "Not a Christian" in the first box, "Christian" in the second, and "Born Again Christian" in the third.

Not a Christian   *Christian*   *Born Again Christian*

Then I ask them to choose which box best describes their spiritual status. Which would you guess most choose? If you said box number two, you are correct. That's because most people I meet with identify either with protestant Christianity or Catholicism, even when it's something from their family's distant past. "Christian" becomes their logical choice.

Then beneath these three boxes I draw three more empty boxes. As I fill these in, I describe the hypothetical scenario of being married and trying to have a child. Then I say, "Supposes your spouse thinks she might be pregnant and decides to go for a pregnancy test." I then describe each of three different findings she could return home to announce.

In the first box, I write "not pregnant." I then move to the third box and write the word "pregnant." Finally, in the middle box I write "semi-pregnant."

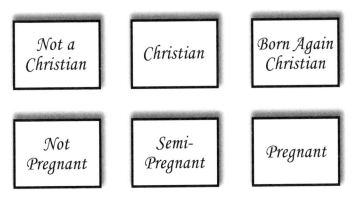

Then I ask my friends what someone would say to his wife if she said she was semi-pregnant. Of course, the answer is, "Honey, I don't think you understand pregnancy." Then I graciously try to explain that when someone says he is a Christian but not born-again, he doesn't quite understand what Jesus taught about being a Christian. To be a Christian is to be born again. The two are synonymous. We just have to get past the "turn-offs" from those who abuse this descriptive term, born again.

We get our initial deposit or infusion of glory at this rebirth. This imputed (placed within) glory has put smiles on many a face. It's responsible for relieving hopelessness and life-threatening depression. It has carried numerous people through years of physical pain and suffering. In Romans, the apostle Paul speaks out of experience when he says, "The sufferings of this present time are not worthy to be compared to the glory that is to be revealed to us."[8] We will discuss this in the final chapter of "The Story of Glory."

For now, I can say with confidence that only the discovery of glory will end your search—or, more appropriately, *should* end your search. The next chapter will explain what I mean.

DEPOSITS AND WITHDRAWALS OF GLORY

In the previous chapter, I described the discovery of glory as our initial deposit of glory that takes place at the point of embracing a relationship with Christ. This glory is what gives birth to satisfaction. As Augustine once prayed, "You made us for Yourself and our hearts find no peace till they rest in You." This is the rest Judy had been longing for.

This newfound glory answers a lifetime of questions as to why nothing other than Christ fully satisfies. Peter Kreeft writes:

The four most salient facts about the human condition are:

+ *All desire perfect happiness.*

+ *No one is perfectly happy.*

+ *All desire complete certainty and perfect wisdom.*

+ *No one is completely certain or perfectly wise.*

The two things we all want are the two things no one has. We behave as if we remember Eden and can't recapture it, like kings and queens dressed in rags who are wandering the world in search of their thrones. If we had never reigned, why would we seek a throne? If we had always been beggars, why would we be discontent? People born beggars in a society of beggars accept themselves as they are. The fact that we gloriously and irrationally disobey the first and greatest commandment of our modern prophets (the pop psychologists)—that we do not accept ourselves as we are—strongly points to the conclusion that we must at least unconsciously desire, and thus somehow remember, a better state.[9]

C.S. Lewis put it this way:

If I find in myself a desire which no experience in this world can satisfy, the most probable explanation is that I was made for another world[10] *…The books or the music in which we thought the beauty was located will betray us if we trust in them…For they are not the thing itself. They are only the scent of a flower we have not found, the echo of a true tune we have not heard, news from a country we have never yet visited.*[11]

Once the flower is found, the tune is heard, and the country is visited, you would think the story ends. Though in part this is true, the reality is that after tasting glory, the flower is only recognized from a distance, the tune is heard without perfect clarity, and the country has much territory yet to be discovered. The Story of Glory continues as we now consider the next chapters: "Deposits and Withdrawals of Glory."

Deposits of Glory

The initial deposit of glory was never intended to be enough. God wants to make additional deposits into our lives every day we live on this earth. The obvious question begging to be answered is, "How do we receive more deposits of glory?"

Oddly enough, we *receive* glory as we *give* glory to the God *of* glory. Scripture repeatedly describes the glory of the Lord. For instance, the Psalmist David says in Psalm 138:5 that "great is the glory of the LORD." Glorifying God is nothing more than applauding God for the glory He has displayed. It is being satisfied with His greatness. This is the source of true happiness. As Jonathan Edwards describes it:

The happiness of the creature consists in rejoicing in God, by which also God is magnified and exalted.

Does this sound complicated? It really isn't. It means that we gain glory from God by giving glory to God. And we give Him glory when we do two things. First, we recognize and renounce all counterfeit glories, declaring them insufficient to satisfy us. Second, we place our only hope for satisfaction in Him. When we do this, the search for meaning and satisfaction is now complete.

The apostle Paul tells us in 2 Corinthians that as we "reflect the Lord's glory," we are "transformed into His likeness with an *ever increasing glory*, which comes from the Lord."[12]

Do you know people who are so satisfied in their relationship with Christ that they could lose everything others value in life and still be content? The Apostle Paul was such a person. I think he was being completely honest when he said,

> *Whatever things were gain to me, those things I have counted as loss for the sake of Christ. More than that, I count all things to be loss in view of the surpassing value of knowing Christ Jesus my Lord, for whom I have suffered the loss of all things, and count them but rubbish in order that I may gain Christ, and may be found in Him, not having a righteousness of my own derived from the Law, but that which is through faith in Christ, the righteousness which comes from God on the basis of faith.[13]*

Jim Elliot was a young man who, at the age of 28, took his wife and young family to the jungles of Ecuador to live. Jim had heard of savage, stone-age killers known as the Aucas living deep in the South American rain forest. Jim's understanding of true life satisfaction created within him a desire to share with the Aucas how they too could find satisfaction.

"He is no fool who gives what he cannot keep to gain what he cannot lose."

Prior to leaving for Ecuador, Jim's friends had challenged his decision to abandon the pursuit of common treasures of this world. Jim's response was, "He is no fool who gives up what he cannot keep to gain what he cannot lose."[14] On a beautiful Sunday afternoon deep in the rain forest on a sandy beach, Jim and his four missionary companions were martyred by the very people they had so desired might come to understand true satisfaction. Jim was focused on the gain of glory.

Once we recognize that we can be satisfied only by acquiring glory, we see the pursuits of this world in a totally different manner. Unfortunately, not all Christians fully embrace this ideal—thus my earlier comment that Christians' search for glory *should* be final. For all of us, to some degree, the search continues unnecessarily. Let me explain.

Withdrawals of Glory

Many Christians—perhaps most—continue to live with faulty reasoning. They think, "If Christ, the hope of glory, gives me satisfaction, think how satisfied I can be with Christ *and* the other things of this world."

What many fail to understand is that the pursuit of other things to satisfy us creates withdrawals of glory. Now don't get me wrong; the "other things" may be good in and of themselves. It's when we embrace them as idols (view them as necessary to be satisfied in life) that they rival the place of God. Such rivals deplete man's glory. Ironically, many a Christian who has all he needs becomes all the more miserable the more he acquires.

The Christian community of our day is filled with impoverished wealthy people—wealthy because they possess Christ, but impoverished because of multiple withdrawals of glory brought about by forsaking the pursuit of Christ alone.

A Time to Pause

Would you consider yourself a Christian? If not, I will explain in detail what is involved in receiving that initial deposit of glory as I develop the second of our three words. But if you do consider yourself a

Christian, let me ask one further question. "Is there something you could lose—or know you could never have—that would leave you dissatisfied with life?" Whatever you identify is the very cause of glory withdrawals.

God's remedy for our idolatry is called repentance. Repentance is admitting that what we have done is wrong, but it goes a step further. Repentance also includes remorse for what has been done—not simply because of the damage done to ourselves, but for the offense brought to our gracious God. But true

> *Repentance is admitting wrong with genuine remorse and returning to the embrace of a loving Father.*

repentance goes even one step further. Repentance is coming back home to the Father. It is embracing His love and acknowledging that He alone is sufficient.

If you're a Christian and bankrupt of glory, this might be a good time to express your repentance to Him and to come home. If so, get ready for further deposits of glory and the sweet satisfaction that follows.

6

FULL OF GLORY

"Full of Glory," the final chapter of "The Story of Glory," is truly the icing on the cake. It can get no better than what we find there. This reality would make Judy's struggle in life a lot more bearable.

Full of Glory

Theologians have a name for what happens when a Christian dies. It's called "glorification." It refers to a state in which a believer is full of glory. The glory of the present, regardless of how many deposits we have made, cannot compare to this fullness of glory eventually to be received. The apostle Paul writes of this glory in 2 Corinthians. "What was glorious has no glory now in comparison with the surpassing glory. And if what was fading away came with glory, how much greater is the glory of that which lasts!"[15]

From the time of the "fall from glory," life remains broken. On earth, Christians can never experience full glory. Yet at death, all that changes. Being aware of this makes the future appear brighter than the present. In the present, the Christian can be satisfied with Christ; however, he cannot be satisfied with life, in and of itself.

Glorification is so wonderful that just the anticipation of it puts all of this world's brokenness into perspective. As I alluded to earlier, Paul describes the contrast between the present and future: "The sufferings of this present time are not worthy to be compared to the glory that is to be revealed to us."[16]

Only a mother knows how painful childbearing is. As awful as my wife describes labor, and as torturous as it appeared to me, only one thing made it tolerable—the hope of the glory of a newborn. The coming baby does not take the pain away, but it sure makes it bearable. In fact, for my wife, it was bearable enough to choose to go through the pain three more times!

Those who are not Christians must face the pain of life without hope of the glory yet to be revealed. Christians who live without thought of the glory are, practically speaking, no better off. Sure, the glory will certainly be theirs; but the hope advantage is forfeited, and the pain of life can seem just as unbearable.

Is life for you extremely painful right now? If so, where are your thoughts focused during these struggles? Do you find yourself consumed with the birth pains of life, or are you focused on the new life promised you for all eternity?

Heaven is described throughout Scripture to remind us just how good "full of glory" really is. It is to our great advantage to stay focused on this truth regarding "the yet to come."

I know this is easier said than done, but it's possible to keep such a focus, and it requires thinking on the truth. As Jesus said, "You shall know the truth and the truth shall make you free."[17] This is the freedom Judy, John, and Charles had been craving for a long time.

The Story's Epilogue

Now you know "The Story of Glory." If space permitted, I could tell you of countless men, women, and students who would say that finding Christ is not only their hope of glory, but their true source of it. Judy is alive and well today because of this glory. John is thriving with a renewed marriage and a passion for bringing glory to God in all of life, especially as a businessman. Charles comes home from school full of hope and purpose as a new follower of Christ.

I know of no single truth as important to me on a day-to-day basis as "The Story of Glory." But there are still two other words that cannot be separated from "glory." These words are vital to fully comprehend our story.

> *You shall know the truth and the truth shall make you free.*

The apostle John, in his description of Christ's incarnation, introduces these two words as they relate to glory. In his gospel we read:

> *The Word became flesh, and dwelt among us, and we beheld His glory, . . . full of GRACE and TRUTH.*[18]

Let me now explain the meaning of our second word, "grace."

PART TWO

The Story of Grace

"Do" vs. "Done"

THE FIRST OF TWO APPROACHES
TO RELATING TO GOD

To say the least, Judy was intrigued with what she had heard. It was as if a seed of hope had been planted with the potential to sprout into a life of meaning and purpose. She was eager to move on to the key question: "How does it become real to me?"

The answer she needed is best summarized in those two words used by John to describe the glory of Jesus, "full of grace and truth." I explained that grace and truth were God's means to give to us the needed commodity of authentic glory.

Now the challenge was to make the conception of grace simple. So as I did with John, Charles, and nearly every person I talk to about spiritual formation, I asked if I could show her a diagram. When Judy responded positively, I pulled out a pencil and piece of paper and began drawing and explaining.

I would love to show you the same diagram that so many find helpful. It looks like this:

We'll let this box represent God.

$$\boxed{God}$$

Everyone who believes in God wants to rightly relate to Him. Or to put it another way, everyone wants God to like them. We want God to be good to us now and especially when we die.

There are only two ways to attempt to relate to God. Every religion falls into one of these two approaches. The first is best captured by the word "performance."

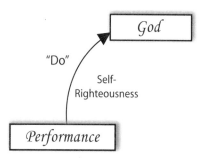

We call this religion "DO." It is based on earning God's favor or affection by what we do or don't do for Him. For this reason, we draw the line *from* the word "performance" *to* the box entitled God.

The interesting reality about such performance is that it does create righteousness. Because this righteousness comes from one's self commitment and determination, we appropriately call it "self-righteousness."

Our immediate reaction to this word is usually negative. Most of us would agree that we dislike self-righteous people. But that's not actually true. In fact, we respect and enjoy self-righteous people. What we really dislike are *haughty*, self-righteous people.

Think about it. If you have children, who do you want them playing with? Kids who act the "right" way. We aren't very concerned about how they got righteous. As long as our kids' friends are not unrighteous, we're happy. We'll accept any variety of righteousness, even the self-made type.

Many of us have been influenced by the teaching of Jesus, who was absolutely repulsed by the self-righteous, so we are quick to reject self-righteousness. Don't be fooled, though. Those self-righteous Scribes and Pharisees would today be highly respected in our society. They would be our conservative community and religious leaders. They would support the causes most beneficial to the well-being of our communities. We would want our children to play with theirs.

So why was Jesus so repulsed by them? The following illustration will perhaps give us some insight.

"You Repulse Me"

Imagine that you are a happily married man. Your wife stops you as you are leaving for work on Monday morning.

"Honey, I want to ask a special favor of you."

You ask her what she wants, but before she answers, she says, "No, promise me before I ask that you will say 'yes'."

In a moment of temporary insanity you say, "I promise," and then brace yourself for what she is about to ask.

"What I want from you is one day of your life. I want a day, preferably a Saturday, to do together anything I choose."

You can only imagine what she might plan, so you ask her what she has in mind.

"I want to awaken early and begin wallpapering our bathroom," she says. "Then at noon, I want to go to the mall and shop until the doors close at 10 p.m."

You think to yourself, "This is the closest description of human hell I have ever heard."

"You will do it, won't you?" she asks. After slowly nodding your head in agreement she says, "How about this Saturday?"

Because you have not yet made plans and you want to get it over with, you say "OK."

Then she says, "Promise you'll keep your word. Tell me that *nothing* will interfere with this Saturday's plans." You assure her of your commitment and leave for the office.

As the week progresses, you find yourself more and more dreading Saturday. When Friday afternoon finally arrives and you prepare to go home, your mind is consumed with your dread of the next day. Then only minutes before leaving the office, you take a phone call from your best golfing buddy.

"Sit down. You're not going to believe what I'm about to tell you," he says.

You can't imagine what could arouse such excitement in his voice. "Let's hear it."

> *You have been invited to play Augusta National!*

"Our lifelong dream has come true. We've been invited to play Augusta National. We're to arrive tomorrow shortly after noon. Can you believe it? It's actually going to happen. We get to play the 'big one'!"

After a moment of silence, he says, "What's wrong? You *can* play, can't you?"

"Of course I can. Even if it costs me my life, I wouldn't miss it." And at the moment, you have no idea just how accurate those words are.

You hang up with contradictory emotions—total exhilaration over the next day's golf plans, but absolute dread of breaking not only the news to your wife but also your promise. As you drive home your mind is racing at a dangerous speed. Necessity once again becomes the mother of invention.

You begin to think to yourself, "What could I do to make this up to her?" Conscious of the fact that you have never given your wife flowers (for *any* occasion), you stop at a florist and buy a beautiful and very expensive arrangement. As you get into the car to head home, it just doesn't feel good enough.

Your mind is still in "creative overdrive," and you notice a jewelry store you must have passed a thousand times without seeing. Then it hits you—now is the time for your first visit to this place of business. Before you leave, you have purchased the necklace you are convinced would make your wife soon forget about an insignificant broken promise.

As you walk into the house, your wife immediately sees the flowers. Assuming they aren't for her, she asks the purpose of the flowers.

"What do you mean?" you say enthusiastically. "They're for you!"

She looks puzzled. "Why? What's the occasion?"

"No occasion. It's just that I've been thinking all week how much I love you and realized how rarely I adequately express how I feel about you. I hope that every time you look at them, you'll remember how much I love you."

With that she runs up to you, throws her arms around your neck, and with a big hug says, "Honey, I can't tell you how happy these flowers make me! I will enjoy them as long as they last."

Now the door is wide open for your next gift. "That's the very point! Those flowers will eventually die, and after buying them I thought to myself, 'Flowers just aren't enough to express how unending my love for you is.' You then hand her the necklace. "I hope this will communicate a little better how much I really love you."

She can't believe her eyes. This time she leaves her feet as she jumps into your arms. And after a passionate kiss unlike any in recent memory, she says, "Sweetie, this is the greatest day of my life." With that the next few hours are spent watching her giddily floating a few feet above ground, happier than you've seen her in years.

After several hours, you decide "if not now, never." It's time to drop the verbal bomb and hope for as little collateral damage as possible.

"Honey, you like the flowers, don't you?"

"More than you'll ever know."

"And what about the necklace?"

"It will forever be my most prized possession."

In hindsight, you might as well have screamed "bomb's away." But instead you simply say, "Sweetheart, there's something I love a lot too." As soon as the word 'golf' leaves your lips, her head cocks with a suspicious look. By the time you get to 'Saturday,' all fury breaks loose.

"So this is what the flowers and necklace are all about! I should have known better!"

With that she takes the flowers out of the vase and throws them in the garbage. She breaks the necklace as she yanks it off her neck and throws it at you, screaming at the top of her lungs, "You repulse me!"

So what happened? Did she suddenly quit liking flowers and necklaces? Of course not. It all had to do with newly recognized motives.

In a similar way, God is repulsed by all the nice things we bring to Him. It's not that He doesn't like our financial gifts, our church attendance, our Bible reading, and our hours of community service. He loves these things—but only when they come from love. God knows our motives, and He is repulsed by the things we do that are designed to make Him like us.

Performance is giving God the things He loves, but with improper motives. To the degree God hates this first approach to relating to Him, however, He loves the second. This is where "grace" comes in.

A SECOND APPROACH TO RELATING TO GOD

THE WORD "GRACE" is placed in our second box. This time, however, the arrow goes *from* God *to* the box titled "grace." Whereas we described the first approach to relating to God using the word "DO," we describe this second approach with the word "DONE."

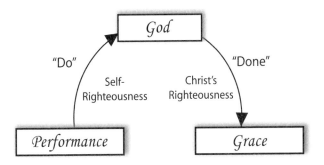

"Grace" is favor merited to us by what God has done for us. When Christ hung on the cross, one of His last statements was, "It is finished." He had DONE what He set out to do-pay for the sins of His followers.

This is what I call "the great swap." Jesus took upon Himself the sins of His people. In exchange, He gives them His perfect righteousness. Paul describes this in 2 Corinthians: "God made Him who knew no sin to be sin on our behalf, that we might become the righteousness of God in Him."[19] Notice I've placed the words "Christ's Righteousness" with the word "DONE."

Peter describes this same swap in his first epistle. "He Himself bore our sins in His body on the cross, that we might die to sin and live to righteousness; For by His wounds you were healed."[20] This righteousness that both Paul and Peter refer to is Christ's righteousness placed in the life of every true follower of Christ. This righteousness is often referred to as "declared righteousness." In other words, a person is declared fully righteous by God the moment this swap takes place.

This doesn't mean we stop sinning, but it does mean that God's sees us as forgiven. God not only likes us now, but in fact loves us unconditionally. Oh, we can still offend Him and even incite His holy anger. But we can never do anything to alter His faithful love for us. He may need to discipline us, but only as a loving father would discipline His children.

This "swap of a lifetime" means that even when we sin we are forgiven. It's true that we must confess our sin to experience the joy and benefits of forgiveness, but we are forgiven solely because of what Christ has done for us.

Once again the Apostle Paul describes this swap—this time in his epistle to the Colossians. There he writes, "And when you were dead in your transgressions and the uncircumcision of your flesh, He made you alive together with Him, having forgiven us all of our transgressions, having cancelled out our certificate of debt consisting of decrees against us and which was hostile to us; and He has taken it out of the way, having nailed it to the cross."[21]

It's as if Jesus, when carrying His cross toward Golgotha, stops for a moment as He sees you or me standing near the roadside. We all have hanging around our necks certificates of debt accounting for every sin ever committed plus those yet to be committed. Seeing one of us, He says, "Randy (or Judy, John, or Charles), give me your certificate."

Curious, we hand it to Him.

Then He says to a centurion, "Can I borrow the mallet you're going to use to nail the spikes into my hands and feet? Can I also have one of your spikes?"

With that, Jesus drives the spike into the certificate laid on the cross. At the moment of His death, our certificate of debt is cancelled and our sins are forgiven. What a deal for you and me.

But the diagram does not end here. The question now is, "So is this just a prayer to receive Jesus, leaving someone free of debt and also free to live however he pleases, forever enjoying eternal security?" Yes and no.

If you mean that the transaction simply means praying a prayer of acceptance, the answer is "no." Prayer may well be the means by which the desire for the swap is communicated, but the prayer must be initiated by a newborn love created in your heart, brought about by this infusion of righteousness (which is based on God's grace). Such an expression of love is called "faith." Faith is trusting in God alone for your righteousness.

What we are describing is a love relationship. A wedding ceremony does not create love between two people. The ceremony is planned *because* of an already existing love relationship. Similarly, a prayer to "receive Christ" doesn't create the love relationship with God. A love relationship birthed in someone's heart creates the desire to invite Him to be master of his or her life.

Note now the conclusion of our diagram.

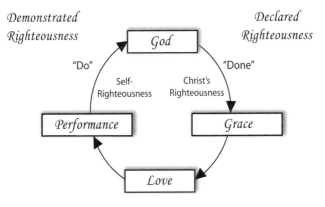

Paul writes in 2 Corinthians, "For Christ's love [for us] compels us [to perform], because we are convinced that one died for all."[22] Christ's love for us compels us to perform. This changes self-righteousness into what's called "demonstrated righteousness." Demonstrated righteousness is always the fruit of "declared righteousness." Without declared righteousness, our best behavior is unacceptable to God (it's called "filthy rags" in Isaiah).[23]

By the way, for those who are familiar with the Bible, this diagram explains what appears to be opposing messages between Paul and James. Paul constantly taught "faith apart from works." James taught "faith without works is dead." I bet you have already solved this apparent contradiction. Paul describes "declared righteousness," which is based solely on the work of Christ. In fact, we can't be declared righteous until we admit that we cannot make ourselves righteous. James argues the importance of "demonstrated righteousness." He goes so far as to say that if you think you have 'declared righteousness' (faith) but have no 'demonstrated righteousness' (works), then you've never received God's righteousness.

Making an Honest Evaluation

At this point, I ask every person I meet with to make an honest evaluation. I ask you to do the same. Where would you say your spiritual pilgrimage begins? Where the dotted line is placed? Or where the solid line is drawn?

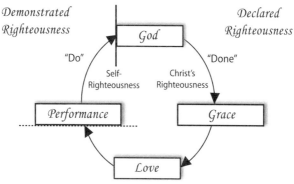

The dotted line represents the beginning of the spiritual pilgrimage of those who may live an attractive, moral, and religious life, but do so *in order* for God to love them. The solid line describes the beginning of the spiritual pilgrimage of those whose life may look outwardly similar. The difference is that they live this way *because* God loves them.

Remember the earlier question on page 37 to which I answered, "yes and no": "So is this just a prayer to receive Jesus, leaving someone free of debt and also free to live as one pleases, forever enjoying eternal security?"

The answer is also "yes." It leaves any true follower not just free from sin's debt, but also free to live *as one pleases*. That's the point. Those who receive Christ's righteousness (born again) are given the moral ability (freedom) to do exactly what they please—that is, to perform for God—but now from being motivated by what God has done.

So which line best describes your spiritual pilgrimage? And, by the way, don't say somewhere in the middle. It's a lot like being "semi-pregnant."

THREE ESSENTIAL BELIEFS

Whether meeting with Judy, John, Charles, or anyone else, it won't be long before they hear me explain three statements. Each statement summarizes a belief that must be embraced in order to move from performance to grace as one's means of relating to God. Let's take a look at these three.

We Lost It All

The first statement is, "We Lost It All." I use the term "we" to refer to all mankind. "All" is in reference to all virtue or goodness.

People who know little or nothing of grace can only presume that good performance before God is their greatest asset in life. After all, doesn't God let good people into heaven? Of course He does. This we would all agree. But where the controversy begins is in agreeing on who is good.

Are you good? Am I good? How good do you have to be to be considered good enough? Ironically, regardless how hard we try to be good, deep down we live with a sense of failure—because we intrinsically know we could be a whole lot better.

If we're honest with ourselves, those of us who try to relate to God by performance have to admit that we live in a constant state of moral failure. And few things fracture a person's sense of well being more than failure.

For several years I served as a chaplain to professional tennis players on tour. One day I asked one of the players, who had won every major tournament on tour and was still highly ranked, how he was doing. His response caught me off guard. "How would you be doing if in your job you were a failure all but three or four weeks a year?"

He explained by saying, "If I have a great year, I win three or four tournaments. Every other week I play, I come home a loser. Oh yeah, I might win two or three rounds in a tournament or perhaps even get beat in the semis or finals. But if you don't win the tournament you ultimately come home a loser. And who likes being a failure all the time?"

Those of us who try to relate to God by performance have to come home every day knowing we lost the battle of perfection. All we're left with is the consolation of comparing ourselves with those who have failed more significantly than we have.

This has been a problem since the day mankind's original parents were stripped of their glory. God didn't want his human creation to be deceived about their perceived goodness. That's why He gave the Ten Commandments and hundreds of other directives related to them.

The New Testament book of Galatians explains that these laws were intended to serve as a type of tutor to point us to the solution necessary to deal with our moral shortfall. Our second statement explains that solution.

He Did It All

Though we lost it all, the good news for mankind is that He, Christ, did it all. "All" refers to everything necessary for lawbreakers like you and me to be pardoned. This is the great swap we talked about in the previous chapter. Because of what Christ does by going to the cross, those who become His followers receive incredible benefits. These benefits are explained by the third and final statement.

We Get It All

The final statement is, "We Get It All." "We" refers to Christ's followers. But what exactly do His followers get? His full righteousness. This includes total forgiveness for all sins—past, present, and future. It means being viewed by God as righteous as Christ Himself is. Because God's righteousness is "imputed" (placed within) the believer, we now have a moral ability to not only do the right thing, but to do those things with the right motives. And it also means that God loves us regardless of what we do. Sure, our sins grieve Him greatly, but only as parents would grieve over their children's faults. With God, our sins never alter His perfectly unconditional love.

Can you imagine living every day of your life assured of being loved by God? "All" includes everything good and everything necessary both to live rightly relating to God and to live life fully satisfied—without need of performance.

But notice the Christians you know. In fact, if you're already a follower of Christ, look at your own life. We probably have to admit that most Christians still believe they must "perform" to keep God's love and approval. The next chapter will help explain why.

10

"SO THAT EXPLAINS MY PERFORMANCE"

Wʜᴀᴛ I ʜᴀᴠᴇ just explained is called "the gospel." Gospel means "good news." But beware. There is a distorted view that has become very popular in this modern day. This distorted gospel, like the authentic one, is summarized by three beliefs—the first being, "We Lost a Lot."

We Lost a Lot

This view of the good news embraces the belief that we lost perfection at the fall of our original parents. But loss of goodness is another matter. This distorted gospel believes that at the fall mankind lost his spiritual health but not his life. Man is therefore born into this world sick and wounded, but not dead in his sin.

In other words, this distorted version suggests that there is a little good in every person. Isn't this what most people believe today, including Christians? Yet the Bible clearly teaches otherwise. Because "all have sinned and fall short of the glory of God,"[24] it's clear that man is not just wounded by his sin, but rather *dead* because of his sin. In fact, Paul writes in Ephesians, "you were dead in your trespasses and sins."[25]

All this explains the teaching of both the psalmist David and the apostle Paul. Paul, quoting David, describes man's moral condition as void of any goodness. We read in Romans, "There is none righteous, not even one; there is none who understands, there is none who seeks for God; all have turned aside, together they have become useless; there is none who does good, there is not even one."[26]

If we are honest, we have to admit that this seems to contradict what we see in people. There are many good people who are not Christians. And if everyone is equally dead in their sins, why are some people so much better than others?

Let me explain with an illustration. My grandfather owned a funeral home. As a child, I would spend time at the funeral home when visiting my grandparents. Most days a corpse was brought to the funeral home for preparation for burial. Some would be brought in within hours of their deaths. I would stare at these lifeless bodies, confused by how alive they looked—as if they were merely asleep. But from time to time, a murder victim would be brought in after being found weeks after death. The decayed body would carry an awful stench.

Now which of these two corpses would be the most dead? The reality is they are equally dead. One has just decayed more than the other. Likewise, all people are dead in their sins. Some, however, have decayed more than others.

Unfortunately, even longtime Christians sometimes don't understand this. Try asking a group of Christians what happens to people of another religion when they die (assuming they've faithfully followed the only religion they knew). Christians find it hard to embrace the teaching of Christ and all of Scripture. The belief that "we lost a lot" logically leads them to assume that there is a little good left in all people, so it seems unfair for a loving God to reject good people of other religions.

In fact, most Christians I talk to who do believe that non-Christians are rightly rejected by God believe they are rejected because they first rejected Jesus. Not so. Were that the case, God would have been obligated to send His Son. And if that were so, Jesus would not be a gift and we would have to do away with the idea of grace. In fact, if this were true, we should fight missionary endeavors. We wouldn't want people to learn about Jesus. Think about it—no knowledge of Jesus would mean no rejection of Jesus. And no rejection of Jesus would mean no rejection by God.

The truth is, if Jesus had never been sent, we would still deserve to be rejected by God. Paul explains this in Romans when he writes, "The wrath of God is revealed from heaven against all ungodliness and unrighteousness of men, who suppress the truth in unrighteousness."[27] None of us is good in and of him- or herself, because we *all* "suppress the truth of God in unrighteousness," leaving none good, "not even one."[28] And since none are good, "there is none who seek for God."[29]

As you can see, there's a big difference between the first belief of the gospel and its distorted version. The dangerous thing about believing that we only lost a lot is its logical implication. The second belief will explain that implication.

He Did a Lot

What exactly did Christ do regarding our salvation? We know He went to the cross, dying for our sins. Without question, that's a lot. And this leads to the second belief of the distorted gospel: "He Did a Lot." According to this version of the gospel, those of us who become Christians take the goodness residing within us and create our required faith and repentance. Thus, the conclusion is that Jesus does His part (a lot) and we do our part.

The authentic gospel says He did it *all*. It attributes even the faith and repentance we exhibit as ultimately a gift of His grace. These are fruits of His regenerating work of placing life within us—all based on grace alone. The authentic gospel has absolutely no room for the meritorious work of self-supplying any aspect of our salvation.

When I first understood the difference between Christ's doing a lot and His doing it all, I was overwhelmed by His love. Luke 7:47 began to take on a greater meaning. Here Jesus says, "He who is forgiven little, loves little."[30] Think about that—only when we believe we lost it all do we believe that Christ must do *everything* for us. And only to the degree that we believe Christ did it all can we understand just how big our forgiveness is. As Jesus taught, the one forgiven much is logically the one who will love much.

But the distorted gospel does not end here. You can now guess its final belief. This final belief explains a lot of our daily behavior.

We Get a Lot

The last belief of the distorted gospel is not the good news you and I long for and need to hear. This belief "We Get a Lot" may sound good, but it's not good enough. The difference between "a lot" and "all" is considerable.

If Christ did not do it all, there's something left for us to do, and that sense of always having "to do" something persists, even after we understand that we got a lot. Sure, we know we get forgiveness of sins, adoption into God's family, and certainty of eternal life. And, in fact, we could list many other things we get. But as long as our beliefs leave us with anything lacking, this becomes the breeding ground for performance.

Only when we believe we get it all, even His full righteousness, can we expect to rest in Him and accept what He did as enough. If you are already a Christian, have you noticed how performance-oriented you are in your relationship with God? Do you find yourself thinking, "If I don't live as I should, God won't love me as much?" Do you ever look at your past moral failures and think that God couldn't—or at least wouldn't— use you because of the terrible things you have done? Do you ever expect things to go bad during days where you failed to spend appropriate time in the morning reading God's Word and praying? These are just a few of many indicators that we are caught in a performance trap.

Where did all this begin? With one simple misbelief—that we only lost a lot. The cause and effect is all too obvious. Embrace the authentic gospel and begin enjoying the freedom God intended you to experience.

One More Word

If you are where Judy, John, and Charles were when I met them, there is still one more word you must understand to find satisfaction in life. It's the word "truth." Remember the verse in John that says, "We beheld His *glory* . . . full of *grace* and *truth*."[31]

PART THREE

The Story of Truth

Truth or Consequences

11

IS THERE SUCH A THING?

Truth. The very word itself is controversial at the least, and at its worst is divisive. Such controversy and division exist because of a deeper issue—a modern-day conflict between the two worldviews of theism and naturalism.

Theism is the belief in a transcendent God who is creator of the universe. Naturalism is the belief that natural causes alone are the reasons for the world as we know it. It's a difference in whether one sees God or the cosmos as the ultimate reality. Is there a God who is absolute—who has revealed His truth to mankind? Or is truth something that man creates for himself?

Jesus talked a lot about truth. He declared Himself and God's Word to be truth. With regards to Himself, He said, "I am the way, the *truth*, and the life."[32] Speaking to His Father, He said, "Your word is *truth*."[33]

From its inception, historic Christianity has held that there is a truth that is discoverable. That truth finds its fullest expression in God. He has chosen to reveal Himself through His Word. Additionally, Christianity maintains that God took an extraordinary step in revealing Himself in the person of Jesus. Jesus, while living, claimed to be one with God and thus the embodiment of truth.

But today in both a post-Christian world (Judeo-Christian truth no longer relied on as the basis of public philosophy or moral consensus[34]) and a post-modern world (resistant to not only Christian truth claims but to *any* truth claims[35]), moral relativism is becoming the norm. If nature's all there is, then there's no transcendent source for moral truth. Every person decides for himself what is moral and what is immoral. What is moral for me may or may not be moral for you.

Allan Bloom, in his book *The Closing Of The American Mind*, says, "There is one thing a professor can be absolutely certain of. Almost every student entering the university believes, or says he believes, that truth is relative."[36] Only 22 percent of adults believe in absolute moral truths. The number goes down to 13 percent from those 36 and under.[37]

In his book *The Grace and Truth Paradox*, Randy Alcorn challenges the logic of those who reject truth as absolute. He mentions four common responses.

The really important thing (so they say) isn't finding the truth; it's searching for it.

Really? Try applying the same logic to your search for a job or parking space—or a flotation device when you're drowning.

There's no such thing as truth.

Is that a true statement? Apparently it can't be. And why would anyone go to college to learn from professors who believe there is no truth?

Truth is whatever you sincerely believe.

You can walk off a ledge sincerely believing you won't fall, but gravity cares nothing about your sincerity. We're not nearly as sincere as we imagine, but even when we are, we're often wrong.

What's true for you is true for you, and what's true for me is true for me.

So, if we step off the roof at the same time, I'll fall because I believe in gravity, but you'll hover in the air because you don't?[38]

Clearly, truth will assert itself the moment one steps off of the roof. The question of truth that each of us has to answer is: "Do I pursue and embrace truth or do I just assume that truth is relative or non-existent?" If the answer is to pursue and embrace truth, then we must investigate Jesus' claim to be God and whether the Bible is God's revelation has merit. If you are uncertain about your beliefs on these issues, let me encourage you to refer to the appendix at the end of this book for some additional resources.

The record of the Bible reveals that God intends for His human creation to experience the satisfaction of glory. As already explained, the glory received at salvation is only an initial deposit. I mentioned earlier that God intends for His people to enjoy additional deposits of glory until finally receiving full glory at death. The route to such additional deposits of glory is found only on the pathway of truth. Only to the degree of embracing God's absolute truth can a Christian expect to enjoy the satisfaction of authentic glory.

With Judy, John, Charles, and almost everyone to whom I explain the claims of Christ, I like to diagram this reality:

Initial Glory — *Deposits of Glory* — *Full Glory*

Truth

Unfortunately, as also mentioned earlier, we all stray off course to varying degrees in pursuit of counterfeit glories. Our departures always take us away from truth. In our next chapter we will identify the pathway to such destructive destinies.

TRUTH'S NUMBER ONE COMPETITOR

Suppose you were married to someone you no longer love. Regardless of your effort, even liking your spouse seems impossible. As a result, eventually your spouse no longer loves you. What does your reason tell you to do?

Let's say an associate at work spreads rumors about you to undermine your integrity and beat you out of a promotion. How does your reason tell you to respond?

Imagine the hardship placed upon you if you found out you were pregnant without a husband and without financial means. You know that your boyfriend, whom you love very much, will desert you as soon as he learns of the pregnancy. Your parents are in favor of terminating the pregnancy and will cover all the costs. To do so will instantly save not only your relationship with your boyfriend but also a good, long-standing reputation in your small hometown community. What response does your reason tell you to take?

Apart from being schooled by the truth of God's Word, reason can be a dangerous enemy. In fact, reason is to truth what performance is to grace—rival worldviews leading to unwanted destinies.

As mentioned in the previous chapter, we all, to varying degrees, stray off course in pursuit of counterfeit glories. Such departures always take us away from truth. And the route to these counterfeit glories is always the same: it's called "faulty reason."

So to complete our diagram, it looks like this:

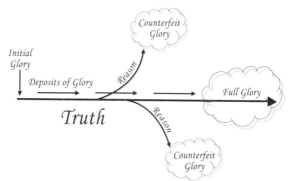

If you or I see something we want badly enough, it's amazing how convincing our reasoning can become. A close Christian friend who had faithfully endured a marriage to a most difficult woman called me to inform me of his recent decision to divorce his spouse, though without biblical grounds. My response was in essence to ask him whether his life commitment was to truth or reason. After a pause, and giving "truth" as his answer, my response was simply to say, "Then you must either change your commitment from truth or change your decision to divorce."

Reason, when left unchecked by God's truth, leads men, women, and children alike to many wrong conclusions:

- ✦ regarding self—such as thinking we are worthless, having no unique value.
- ✦ regarding God—such as thinking, "Since I love people too much to send them to hell, and since God surely loves them more than I do, He would never send a person to such punishment."
- ✦ regarding possessions—such as being convinced that great wealth is a ticket to a happy and satisfied life.

I could go on and on. But having said all of this, let me make it clear that as dangerous as reason can be, it isn't wrong in and of itself. It is only as reason departs from truth that it becomes so deceitful.

Neither is truth in any way to be viewed as unreasonable. At first look, some of God's thoughts seem to be everything but reasonable. But that should be no surprise. As Isaiah records, "My thoughts are not your thoughts, neither are your ways My ways. . . . As the heavens are higher than the earth, so are My ways higher than your ways, and My thoughts than your thoughts."[39] And as Moses writes, "The secret things belong to the LORD our God, but the things revealed belong to us and to our sons forever, that we may follow all the words of this law."[40]

But upon further examination we begin to realize that every directive God gives us in His word is for one of three reasons: to protect us from someone else, to protect others from us, or to protect us from ourselves.

Much of what we see in Scripture is paradoxical. It seems to be contradictory on the surface, but when we dig deeper, we find that it isn't. Other writings of Scripture are merely mystery—beyond our comprehension. Even in this modern world, we have examples of embracing what we can't understand. For instance, think about black holes in the universe. We know they are there, but can you explain them?

So, yes, there is biblical paradox and there is mystery. But what we *never* find in God's Word is contradiction.

If there is any single issue which is raised most often against the truth of God's Word, it has to be that of evolution. After all, doesn't the Bible clearly say that the world was created? And doesn't science prove that the world evolved? If so, then at least on this issue, God's supposed truth is at best unreasonable, and at worst not true.

We'll talk about evolution later on. But first, let's look at the contrast between where truth and reason eventually take us.

FREEDOM OR BONDAGE

During His teaching ministry, Jesus made a bold claim about the impact of truth: "You shall know the truth and the truth shall set you free."[41] So the byproduct of truth is the all-important commodity of freedom.

On the other hand, God's Word repeatedly teaches that to deny truth is to ultimately experience bondage. The author of Proverbs tells us, "There is a way that seems right to a man, but in the end it leads to death."[42]

In Matthew 7, Jesus teaches of two ways, one broad and the other narrow. The broad way is entered through a wide gate and is filled with large numbers of travelers. This way, though perhaps appearing to be reasonable, leads to destruction.

On the other hand, the narrow way is entered through a small gate and has much fewer people traveling it. We could perhaps assume by the fact of its fewer travelers that this second way doesn't seem as reasonable to travel as the other road. This road, however, leads to life.

According to Jesus one of the byproducts of Truth is freedom.

That's exactly why we need truth, not reason, to direct our daily lives. The issue really is one of trust. Can we rely on what God's Word says to be truth? Can we be certain that truth really does always lead to freedom?

Many today will say that the very reason they don't want to follow God's Word is that they want freedom. They don't want to be told what they can or can't do. They want to make their own choices.

Unfortunately, such comments indicate a misunderstanding of the concept of freedom. What they are embracing is not freedom, but rather a deceitful imposter called license.

License is the opportunity to do whatever one wishes whenever one wishes. Freedom is not the opportunity to do what one wants to do, but rather the ability to do what one *should* do.

Imagine a train that can feel and talk like a person. As it heads down a mountain range, it grumbles about the long journey required by the track. It then decides it wants to be free from its track and to go straight down the mountainside. It's thrilled not only with the time it can save, but even more with the rush of the adventure. All would agree that such license will lead to anything but freedom. In fact, it would lead to destruction. Those tracks, as confining as they may appear, are the very means for the freedom necessary to take the train to its safe destiny.

So we see God's Word both assuring freedom to those who follow truth and warning of bondage to those who depart from it.

We also see this in every day life. For instance, Scripture warns parents not to train up their children in the way they choose to be trained, lest they never depart from it (Proverbs 22:6). And experience proves that children who are taught to embrace the morals of Scripture with the right motives will experience successes in life that those who reject such teaching do not enjoy.

There is perhaps no more dramatic illustration of this than in the story of two families—that of Jonathan and Sarah Edwards and a family we will call the Jukes.

Jonathan Edwards, believed by many to be the greatest pastor in American history, lived in the 1700s. The Jukes family originated from one immigrant who settled in upstate New York in 1720. The Jukes family had no commitment to the truth of God's Word. The Edwards, on the other hand, held strongly to God's revelation as the only source of infallible truth.

In 1900, A.E. Winship tracked down 1,400 of the Edwards' family descendants and a similar number of the Jukes' descendants. He then published a study of these two families in contrast to one another.

A summary of this report is found in a book written about Jonathan and Sarah Edwards by Elizabeth Dodds.[43] The contrast between the two families illustrates the bondage that departing from God's truth brings and the fruit of freedom that results from adhering to it.

Dodds writes:

Winship learned that a descendant of the Edwardses presided over the New York Prison Commission in 1874 when it conducted an inquiry into the Jukes matter. Only 20 of the 1,200 Jukes had ever had gainful employment (the others were either criminals or lived on state aid), whereas the Edwards family had contributed astonishing riches to the American scene. "Whatever the family has done it has done ably and nobly," Winship contended.

By 1900, when Winship made his study, this single marriage had produced:

13 college presidents
65 professors
100 lawyers and a dean of an outstanding law school
30 judges
66 physicians and a dean of a medical school
80 holders of public office:
three United States senators
mayors of three large cities
governors of three states
a vice president of the United States, and
a controller of the United States Treasury.

Almost all the men had college degrees and many completed graduate work in a time when this was unusual. The women were repeatedly described as "great readers" or "highly intelligent," although girls were not sent to college then. Members of the family wrote 135 books. They edited eighteen journals and periodicals. They entered the ministry in platoons and sent one hundred missionaries overseas, as well as stocking many mission boards with lay trustees. One maverick married the daughter of a South Sea Island chieftain, but even that branch reverted to type, and its son became a clergyman. As Winship put it:

"Many large banks, banking houses, and insurance companies have been directed by them. They have been owners or superintendents of large coal mines...of large iron plants and vast oil interests...and silver mines...There is scarcely any great American industry that has not had one of this family among its chief promoters...The family has cost the country nothing in pauperism, in crime, in hospital or asylum service; on the contrary, it represents the highest usefulness."

The line still continues to be vigorous, intelligent, and enlivening to society. Yet all this achievement came out of a family with no large inherited fortune. All the children's accomplishments were the result of their personal initiative.[44]

As strongly as the Bible and even life experiences argue for the existence of an absolute truth given by God, all such reasoning is silenced by one theory if proven. And I bet you've already figured out that I'm referring to evolution. So let's take a look at this popular belief.

14

WHAT ABOUT EVOLUTION?

W HILE HAVING LUNCH recently with a man who was investigating Christianity, he informed me that while he believed most of the Bible, he certainly couldn't accept its teaching on creation. When I asked him why he couldn't believe in creation, his response was what I expected: "Because science has proven otherwise."

This led to a discussion that I always enjoy. I asked him what he would think under the following scenario: "Assume you lived at a time when there was no such thing known to you as a clock or watch. One day while walking on a seashore, you find a strange device lying in the water's edge partly covered in sand. As you pick it up, you notice numbers that routinely change at precisely the same amount of time intervals. There are buttons strategically placed on this device that, when pressed, either cause numbers to change or alarm noises to sound. You notice that the device has a strap with a latch device that allows it to be loosened or tightened. Finally, you notice words of some language etched in the metal backing. What would be the likelihood that this item had a designer?"

The answer was obviously, "100 percent certainty." We innately know that design always requires a designer.

At this point I posed several questions. First I asked, "Why do you believe that something so intricately designed as this world and especially human beings would be without a designer?"

"Because science proves it to be otherwise."

Then I asked, "Who told you science proved this?"

His response was that his teachers had always taught him this.

Finally, I asked him if he had ever read any books written by respected scientists and scholars who reject evolution and embrace the belief of creation. Not only had he not done so, but he wasn't aware that any even existed.

Of course, his comment "because science proves it to be otherwise" made no distinction between the creation of intelligent life and that of the universe's existence. However, any evidence of an honest investigation was conspicuously absent. Whether it is the creation of life or of the universe, years of education have predisposed him to accept an answer without the need to investigate on his own.

I then gave him both a challenge and a prediction that I've given to many—and give to you also, if you've believed as my friend. I challenged him to read one or two books detailing the scientific evidence that supports creation. My prediction to him, as it is to you, was that after doing so, he would most likely no longer be as convinced of evolution. By the way, my recommendations for the best books to read on this subject are included in the appendix of this book.

The evidences of cosmology, physics, astronomy, biochemistry, and biological infrastructure (DNA), to name just a few, become overwhelming as to the reasonableness of the truth of creation. Naturalism cannot exist as a worldview apart from a belief in evolution. This explains the inexhaustible effort on behalf of naturalists to prove this false theory.

But in every realm of life, as in the seemingly reasonableness of evolution, the same is always true. When all is said and done, we find that reason, apart from the truth revealed in God's Word, is itself that which is unreasonable. The more I engage in conversations with people on this topic I am more convinced that the "who" of creation is a superior discussion to the "how" of creation.

If you think evolution has been effective at challenging the truth of God's Word, wait till you read the next chapter.

A WORD TO POSTMODERNS

As a Christian with deep conviction who embraces truth and argues for it passionately, I have been accused of intolerance more than a few times. My response is always the same. It goes something like this:

"John, don't you ever call me intolerant! Feel free to call me wrong or even stupid, but don't call me intolerant."

I make my point with an illustration:

Suppose we're having lunch at a restaurant and I excuse myself to go to the restroom. As I walk past the kitchen, I overhear a cook making hateful comments about you to a waiter. I pause to listen to the conversation. The cook says he's prepared to end your life. As he says this, he takes the batter for some cookies and places a large portion of cyanide in the mix and asks the waiter to deliver them to you as an anonymous gift. I can't believe my ears.

I then go immediately back to the table, assuming what I heard couldn't be true. But sure enough, in about the time necessary to bake the cookies, that same waiter arrives at the table explaining that someone anonymously wanted to give these cookies to you.

You are pleasantly surprised and say "Thanks." You then reach for a cookie, and I say, "Don't eat that cookie!" You ask me why not, and I explain what I have just heard. You find this too hard to believe, and you tell me you think I'm crazy. With that, you reach for the cookie.

At this point I say to my accuser, "What do you think I should do under those circumstances?" His response is just what I expect. "You should stop me from eating it." Then I say to him, "Isn't that being intolerant?"

Of course it's not. It's actually an expression of love to insist upon something that will benefit others when we know we have information they don't have (whether right or wrong).

You see, I may have misinterpreted what the cook said and may have mistaken food coloring as poison. But until I know differently, it should never be considered intolerant to insist on what I believe to be true.

Insisting on truth, however, is not a popular stance in a postmodern culture. Over time, Western society has developed a flawed philosophy that keeps us from finding the answers people like Judy, John, and Charles so desperately seek. Perhaps knowing how we got to this point will help expose some of the flaws in our cultural worldview.

In Chapter 11, I introduced the modern-day conflict between the two worldviews of theism and naturalism and explained naturalism as the belief that natural laws alone explain the world as we know it. Naturalism is part of a more comprehensive worldview known as modernism.

The dominant worldview for about two centuries, modernism focused not on God but on humanity. The individual became the highest arbiter of truth, human progress became the ultimate goal, and universal absolutes gave way to the personal pursuit of happiness.

With a human-centered, individualistic approach to truth and purpose in life, it's not hard to see how human relationships deteriorated over time. The dark side of modernity has resulted in wrecked families, a loss of intimacy, and alienation from God and others.

Modernist culture is now evolving into post-Christian and postmodern culture, in which Judeo-Christian truth—or any thought of an absolute truth, for that matter—is rejected as the basis for society's moral consensus.

It's important for us to understand this cultural philosophy, because it explains why we react the way we do when hearing claims about what is true and what is not. We can't find answers in life if we accept our culture's spin on the validity of answers—that truth is relative and a matter of individual preference. Postmodernism denies that we can really know anything about who God is.

> *We cannot find answers in life if we accept our culture's spin on the validity of answers.*

That's why postmodernism is fundamentally opposed to the Christian gospel. Because truth is relative and a matter of individual preference, it cannot provide any sure foundation or markers along life's highway to guide those seriously seeking answers to their questions.

Postmodernism is a natural byproduct of existentialism, a philosophy that views life as meaningless and absurd. If an individual influenced by these worldviews wants any meaning to this life, he'll have to create it by the choices he makes. "Choice" becomes the ultimate value and the single justification for any action.

Postmodernism defines society in terms of gender, ethnicity, and class. Thus we have the birth of a new value—multiculturalism—which is not really about appreciating unique cultures, but about placing the status of the individual in the context of a more important tribal group.

The result is that we now live in a dominant culture that accepts no objective, universal, absolute truth, but believes that truth for that particular group is determined by that group (whether African-American, female, gay, Hispanic, etc.). All viewpoints, lifestyles, beliefs, and even behaviors are viewed as equally valid.

It's easy to see where this takes us. Since historic Christianity holds to truth, it is often accused of intolerance. For the postmodern, tolerance is the ultimate value—so important, in fact, that no exception is tolerated! (Actually, there is one objective truth acceptable in postmodernism: Darwinism, or evolution. But that seems to be the only exception to an otherwise complete rejection of absolutes.) That's why the discussion at the beginning of this chapter is repeated so often.

What does "tolerance" mean for someone looking for answers? If your truth is yours and my truth is mine, then no one's truth is greater than another's. No ideal is worthy of one's costly passion, certainly not enough to fight or die for.

If there is no truth superior to another's truth, then no one can persuade another by rational arguments. The only hope for winning is by the force of power. Since all principles and convictions are merely expressions of personal preference, any appeal to them is seen as a power play, an attempt to impose one's view upon another—a repulsive idea to a postmodernist.

That's why postmoderns are generally resentful of moral absolutes. Absolutes fly in the face of everything they have learned in life through their formal and informal education and have accepted as their belief system. Nature becomes sacred. Self-actualization and spiritual growth are valued—but only as perceived by that individual or group. Hierarchy is devalued. Decentralization, democracy, and egalitarianism are fully embraced.

In all of this confusion and ambiguity is there any hope for those sincerely looking for answers? Some postmoderns are now beginning to see the inadequacy of their beliefs as they recognize the social chaos bred by naturalists. Many are becoming disillusioned by their false beliefs and are beginning to seek real answers to the questions their life experience raises.

One of the most effective counters to the postmodern worldview is the Incarnation, the Son of God taking on of human form and nature. Michael Kruger writes that the Incarnation "is the decisive challenge to postmodernity. One look at Jesus of Nazareth shatters the notion that we can be 'gods' shaping our own reality and truth. The real God has revealed Himself. He has entered the world and walked among us."[45]

Eventually, everyone must decide what to do with Jesus. History validates His life. Time and experience validate His message. Either He truly is "the way, the truth, and the life," or there is no such thing as truth.

If you are a seeker, one who is searching for spiritual answers for the questions of life, be careful when you think one of us is intolerant. Call us wrong, or even call us stupid. But please don't call us intolerant.

There's much more to say about worldviews. I recommend for your reading a work that will take you much further in your understanding of this subject: *How Now Shall We Live* by Charles Colson. Much of what I've said about post-Christian and postmodern culture merely parrots what Colson says in this great book.

But now it's time to see how important this teaching about truth really is. Let's look at the common and extremely powerful reality of depression and see what happens when it encounters objective, absolute truth.

WHEN DEPRESSION ENCOUNTERS TRUTH

My daughter Rachael could not have been a happier child. She was truly the life of every party—as outgoing as anyone you could meet. Rachael entered into high school at the same time we relocated our home and our church. Her new school was not the one that her friends who lived near our old home would attend. Though it was an extremely large public school and she would know very few students, Rachael looked forward to the new adventure—and especially to the new friends she would make. After all, she had rarely met a stranger. However her high school experience did not turn out to be what she expected.

Within a few weeks, Rachael began to discover that not everyone held her beliefs. She struggled in her relationships and began to question herself and God's truth which lead to a downward spiral of depression.

It happened so abruptly. One day Rachael was our happy, smiling girl, and the next she was in deep depression of the ugliest kind. She would have seen death as a welcome friend.

No one was shocked more by this turn of spirits than Rachael herself. I can remember her questioning why God would allow it to happen. After all, she had been faithfully following the Lord. She was consistent in spending ample time with Him in personal worship. She was involved in a discipleship group and frequently participated in service and compassion projects.

Rachael's depression continued for a year and a half. A change of schools, counseling, and even medication seemed to have little effect.

Her turning point began after a very risky conversation with her mother and me.

One evening I asked Rachael to join Carol and me in the family room. As we sat on our couch, I announced to Rachael that I thought I knew the answer to her problem. At this point, she would have welcomed any optimism, but what she heard came as a total shock.

"Rachael," I began, "I think that in order to start getting better, you need to go out and raise hell!" I then suggested a few specific activities for her to begin with. My serious tone of voice let her know Dad was not teasing. Besides, we all knew that this was no laughing matter.

"Dad, how can you say this?" she said. "You've always taught me not to do those things. Why are you saying this?"

I took the opportunity to make my point.

"Rachael, I'm saying this because I'm afraid that's what it will take to show you just how sinful you are." I didn't actually want her to do these things, but I knew it would have been better than the alternative. She was shocked and asked me to explain.

"Rachael, I've heard you say over and over this past year how ugly you are. If Jesus were to walk into this room right now and I were to ask Him if He thought you were ugly, how do you think He would answer? Do you think He'd say, 'Randy, my apologies. I do have to admit that your daughter is one ugly girl'?"

"He would say that I am pretty," she said sheepishly.

"So which do you think offends God the most: the sinful activities I encouraged you to explore, or calling your Designer and Creator either wrong or dishonest about His opinion of you?"

She had to admit that denying the truth about herself was the greater offense.

I then listed some other distortions of the truth Rachael had embraced. Each came from listening to her feelings instead of God's Word. False reason had won over truth, and the result was emotional bondage.

We dealt with this sin just as we would deal with any other sin—by means of repentance. As mentioned earlier, repentance is not merely admitting one's sin, nor is it admitting it with remorse. True repentance is not complete until we come back to the loving arms of our forgiving Father, acknowledging that His love is enough.

> *False reason had won over truth, and the result was emotional bondage.*

In Rachael's case, repentance meant admitting that His love alone was enough—with or without the acceptance of her peers.

This marked the beginning of Rachael's deliverance from depression. It certainly wasn't a one night recovery. It was a process of learning how to think on the truth. Or as the apostle Paul says, "taking every thought captive to the obedience of Christ."[46]

Several years later, I taught a series at our church on depression. Rachael graciously accepted my invitation to tell her story during one of my messages. Her counsel to all was the same as the counsel her mom and I gave her: "Think on the truth." After all, Jesus had promised: "You shall know the truth, and the truth shall make you free."[47]

Having shared Rachael's story, it's important to note that all battles with depression are not the same. There are numerous types. Depression can be caused totally by a chemical imbalance, side effects from medication, glandular disorders, or hormonal irregularities. Some people experience what's called physical depression, which could be caused by an infection of the brain or even improper diet and exercise. Others experience a grief depression, the result of total emotional exhaustion.

But Rachael had been diagnosed with the kind of depression most people experience—circumstantial depression. This type is caused by a pattern of thinking that reflects a wrong or negative view of self, God, the world, or one's future. Circumstantial depression is evidence that one's source of security is misplaced. In essence, it's the result of believing lies—usually heard from within more loudly than from without.

When false reason encounters bad circumstances, depression is often the byproduct. But the good news is that when circumstantial depression encounters truth, depression never has a chance.

Perhaps you're depressed right now. If so, find out what kind of depression you're fighting, and if it's circumstantial, take Rachael's advice—think on the truth!

A Few Final Thoughts

A DANGEROUS BUT SATISFYING JOURNEY

To FOLLOW CHRIST is to embark on a very satisfying journey. At the same time, it is a wild, unpredictable, and even dangerous journey. Please don't think of it as a self-improvement program, a philosophy, or even a religion. It is much more than that.

Like most great adventures, it is a call away from security—in this case, human security. It includes numerous hardships, risks, fears, dislikes, and dangers. But in the end, as in so many adventurous journeys, there are great rewards. The greatest of the rewards is authentic glory—splendor, renown, and satisfaction.

In *The Lion, The Witch, and the Wardrobe*, C. S. Lewis' well-known work for children, Jesus Christ is depicted as a lion named Aslan. Lucy asks Mr. and Mrs. Beaver about him:

"Is he—quite safe? I shall feel rather nervous about meeting a lion."

"That you will dearie and make no mistake," said Mrs. Beaver. "If there's anyone who can appear before Aslan without their knees knocking they're either braver than most or just plain silly."

"Then he isn't safe?" said Lucy. "Safe?" said Mr. Beaver; "Don't you hear what Mrs. Beaver tells you? Who said anything about being safe? Of course he isn't safe. But he's good. He's the King, I tell you."[48]

We must understand both. He is good, but He's not safe. As Randy Alcorn writes in *The Grace and Truth Paradox*, "Until we come to grips with the truth of His uncompromising holiness, we'll never begin to grasp His grace."[49]

In yet another work of Lewis, *The Voyage of the Dawn Treader*, we read of a bright white Lamb speaking in a "sweet milky voice." But all of a sudden, "his snowy white flushed into tawny gold and his size changed and he was Aslan himself, towering above them and scattering light from his mane."[50] The lamb of grace described in Isaiah 53:7 becomes the lion of truth who in Scripture is called the Lion of Judah.

The very naming of Jesus gives us much insight into how "unsafe" Jesus would be. In ancient times, everyone knew that whoever does the naming assumes the role of manager over the one being named. We see this as Adam represented mankind in naming the animals. When kings were defeated, they were given new names by the conquering king. And, of course, parents who name their children must manage them through their early years.

But when we come to the account of Jesus' birth in Matthew 1, Joseph and Mary would not be allowed to name Him. Why, because only the Almighty could manage Him.

You and I must learn that we cannot manage Jesus. He manages us. We cannot have Him as we want Him. We can't follow Him on our own terms. We cannot designate Him as our eternal security blanket. Jesus is no house cat. He's the Lion of Judah. If you try to manage Him, you'll get hurt.

Some say, "But if I submit to Him, I'll have to change the way I live." Of course you will! Some say, "But He might ask me to do things I don't want to do or stop doing things I love." You better believe it.

Even so, let me urge you not to be managed by anyone or anything other than Jesus. Perhaps you're being named and managed by your work, a relationship, a pleasure, your reputation, or your possessions. None of these will meet your need to be loved, but Jesus will. Remember, He may not be safe but He is good. And His love is all you need, because He alone is the hope of glory.

So, in the short term, there's nothing more dangerous than obediently following Him. In the long run, there is nothing more dangerous than ignoring Him—or even playing around with Him on your own terms. Remember, "He is the King, I tell you!"

ADVICE TO SEEKERS

In Chapter 15, I suggested that the greatest challenge to the postmodern is the incarnation of Christ. If Jesus is truly God-man, then we can't determine our own reality. If He isn't God-man, then perhaps our greatest hope is to view ourselves as "gods" determining our own existence. When all is said and done, it comes down to who Jesus is.

C.S. Lewis, noted English author, scholar, and professor, was an agnostic for many years. While an agnostic, he investigated the person of Jesus from an intellectual perspective. After much research, he determined Jesus to be God and became one of His followers.

Lewis believed that everyone should have the opportunity to investigate the person of Jesus. He was convinced that the results of such an investigation can lead to only one of three conclusions.

To believe that Jesus was merely a legend, according to Lewis, was not an intellectually acceptable option. Historical evidence silences proponents of this persuasion. There are only three remaining options. First, perhaps He was a liar, claiming to be God and knowing He wasn't. Second, He could have been a lunatic, believing He was God while in reality being only a man. Or, He was exactly who He claimed to be, Lord of the universe.

Lewis makes this statement:

I am trying here to prevent anyone saying the really foolish thing that people often say about Him. "I'm ready to accept Jesus as a great moral teacher, but I don't accept His claim to be God." That is the one thing we must not say. A man who was merely a man and said the sort of things Jesus said would not be a great moral teacher. You must make a choice. Either this man was and is the son of God or else a madman or something worse.[51]

Years ago, when seeking to arrive at my own convictions about Jesus, I reasoned that if my investigation led me to believe that Jesus was a liar or a lunatic, then I would be a fool to follow Him. But, on the other hand, if my investigation led me to believe He was Lord of the Universe, I'd be a fool of fools not to follow Him.

But how does someone investigate Christ? Obviously, the best place to start is the Bible. But these days when time is such a precious commodity, few of us can take the time for a lengthy, personal investigation. And even if we had the time, most of us would not know where to begin. We would probably start reading in the first book of the Bible, Genesis, stumble through a bunch of "begats," continue in Leviticus and read about a lot of animals getting killed, and then hit Deuteronomy and find a thousand seemingly irrelevant things not to do. Ultimately, we'd probably set the Bible down and conclude we just can't understand it.

In addition to all of this, most people don't like to be preached to, especially about religion. I know I'd rather be given data—brief data—and have the opportunity to read it on my own in the privacy of my home or office. Then all I'd want is a credible person of reference to whom I could honestly push back, ask questions, and get some clarification.

Years ago, it seemed to me that what was needed was a type of "CliffsNotes™" concerning the critical issues of an investigation. Like most sensible students, I would always take the trade off of 90 percent of the information for 10 percent of the time and effort. So I wrote four brief booklets titled "Life Issues," which were designed to help a person in his or her investigation. These booklets have since become widely used both nationally and internationally.

Each booklet deals with one of four critical questions. The first responds to the question, "How can Christians believe that the Bible, written so many years ago, is a perfect writing coming from God and without error. And even if it were given perfectly, how can they believe it has remained without error over all these years?" The second booklet addresses the question, "How can Christians believe that all people, including moral and religious people outside of Christianity, deserve eternal punishment?" The third booklet deals with the question, "How can Christians claim that among all the religious leaders, Jesus Christ is the only way to God?" And the fourth booklet answers the question, "What did Jesus teach was required to have eternal life?"

I am convinced that researching the answers to these four questions is sufficient to conduct an intelligent investigation.

Answers to each question are kept to about seven pages (truly a "CliffsNotes™" size). Each booklet includes five or six chapters of the gospel of John with questions in the margins. The answer to each question is found in the text across from the questions, which aids one's understanding as the passage is read.

Ideally, these booklets are read over four weeks—one booklet a week. I have found that the best investigation includes reading the section of John a little every day throughout the week (rather than once a week at one sitting). And even more importantly, it helps to meet with a mature Christian each week to ask questions concerning the information read. Regardless of how it's done, there's nothing more important than pursuing a careful investigation.

I've often asked those with whom I am sharing the claims of Christ what odds they would place on Jesus being the Son of God. The most common answer I get is "50-50."

If there were only a 10 percent chance of winning a multi-million dollar lottery, would you make the financial investment of purchasing a ticket? Of course you would, even with the odds being so low.

Why, because the payoff is so large compared to the investment. Imagine the payoff if Jesus truly is Lord of the universe. A month's investigation is, in comparison, a very small investment.

I can only assume that every person who believes there is any chance whatsoever of Jesus being God would want to know, when on his deathbed, that he had at least investigated the person of Jesus.

As mentioned earlier, when all is said and done it comes down to who Jesus is. I hope you have already or will soon answer this most important question for yourself.

If you would be interested in getting the four booklets entitled "Life Issues," you can purchase them online at www.LifeonLife.org.

ADVICE TO BELIEVERS

I HAVE THE same routine each morning when I wake up. I get on my knees and pray a very short prayer. Though I'll have a longer season of prayer a little later, this is the most important prayer of the day. It goes like this:

Lord, grant me today to
seek authentic <u>glory</u>,
by means of <u>grace</u> alone,
according to the <u>truth</u> of Your Word.

Then I take a few moments to consider the meanings and implications of what are, for me, the most important three words in the Bible—glory, grace, and truth.

Glory takes me to Christ.

Grace takes me to the Cross.

Truth takes me to the Word of God.

Show me someone whose life stays focused on Christ, His work, and His Word, and I'll show you a satisfied person. That's certainly my story.

Let me encourage you to use this prayer for at least 21 consecutive days—the number of days some say is necessary to establish a habit. The prayer is certainly not magical, but to live out this resolve is to have discovered the answer to life's greatest longing—satisfaction.

APPENDIX

Additional Reading Material on Creation and Evolution

Michael Behe, *Darwin's Black Box: The Biochemical Challenge to Evolution*. New York: The Free Press 1996.

William Lane Craig and Quentin Smith. *Theism, Atheism, and Big Bang Cosmology.* New York: Oxford University Press 1993.

William A. Dembski. *The Design Revolution: Answering the Toughest Questions About Intelligent Design* Downers Grove, IL: InterVarsity Press 2004

Michael Denton. *Evolution: A Theory in Crisis*. Bethesda, MD: Adler & Adler, 1985.

Hank Hanegraaff. *The Face that Demonstrates the Farce of Evolution*. Nashville, TN: Word Publishing 1998.

Phillip E. Johnson.

Darwin on Trial 2nd ed. Downers Grove, IL: InterVarsity Press 1993.

Defeating Darwinism: By Opening Minds. Downers Grove, IL: InterVarsity Press 1997.

Lee Strobel. *The Case for a Creator: A Journalist Investigates Scientific Evidence That Points Toward God.* Grand Rapids, Michigan: Zondervan 2004

Additional Reading Material on Truth

William Edgar, *Lifting the Veil: The Face of Truth*. Phillipsburg, NJ: P&R Publishing 2001.

Phillip E. Johnson.

Reason in the Balance: The Case Against Naturalism in Science, Law & Education. Downers Grove IL: InterVarsity Press 1995.

The Wedge of Truth: Splitting the Foundation of Naturalism. Downers Grove, IL: InterVarsity Press 2000.

WITH GRATITUDE

This project moved from presentations to manuscript because of the not-so-gentle prod of Phil Orazi. Phil serves at Perimeter Church as an Elder and a lay leader for our Arab speaking global outreach ministry. As we traveled through Iraq together and he heard this content being shared with pastors, he insisted that I pull this together in a book to be shared with a broader audience. Thanks to his encouragement and generous support *The Answer* is a resource that I hope will find its way into many hands.

Thanks to Bill Wood, friend, neighbor and church staff peer who has worked with me in every phase of bringing this book to publication. Without Bill's serving heart and diligent hard work, I wonder if this work would have ever been completed. I also want to thank Zoe Huff, one of our staff members at Perimeter Church, for jumping in on this project and providing some great design assistance and managing many of the production details.

ABOUT THE AUTHOR

Randy Pope is the lead teaching pastor of Perimeter Church in Duluth, Georgia. He and his family moved to Atlanta in 1977 to plant Perimeter Church. In the 29 years since then, Perimeter has served thousands of members, has helped plant 24 other churches in the Atlanta area, helped start six training centers worldwide to facilitate church planting, and has partnerships with nationals in 11 countries to help train leaders for the church.

Randy is a graduate of the University of Alabama and Reformed Theological Seminary. He has trained church leaders throughout the world and has been a guest lecturer at numerous graduate schools throughout the U.S. He is the author of two other books: *The Intentional Church* previously released as *The Prevailing Church* and *Finding Your Million Dollar Mate.*

FOOTNOTES

1. Webster's New World Dictionary of the American Language 1969 Edition.

2. Ibid.

3. Blaise Pascal, Pensées W.F. Trotter, translator, (Grand Rapids, MI: Christian Classics Ethereal Library), p. 65.

4. ESV, Psalm 16:4.

5. NAS, John 1:1-2.

6. NAS, John 1:14.

7. NAS, Colossians 1:27.

8. NAS, Romans 8:18.

9. Peter Kreeft & Ronald K. Tacelli, Pocket Handbook of Christian Apologetics, (Downers Grove,IL: InterVarsity Press, 2003), p. 48-49.

10. C.S. Lewis, Mere Christianity, (San Francisco: Zondervan Publishing House, 1980) pp. 136-137.

11. C.S. Lewis, The Weight of Glory (San Francisco: Zondervan Publishing House, 1980) pp. 30-31.

12. NIV, 2 Corinthians 3:18.

13. NAS, Philippians 3:7-19.

14. Elisabeth Elliot, Shadow of the Almighty (San Francisco: Harper & Row, 1979), p. 15.

15. NIV, 2 Corinthians 3:10-11.

16. NAS, Romans 8:18.

17. NAS, John 8:32.

18. NAS, John 1:14.

19. NAS, 2 Corinthians 5:21.

20. NAS, 1 Peter 2:24.

21. NAS, Colossians 2:13-14.

22. NIV, 2 Corinthians 5:14.

23. NAS, Isaiah 64:6.

24. NAS, Romans 3:23.

25. NAS, Ephesians 2:1.

26. NAS, Romans 3:10-12.

27. NAS, Romans 1:18.

28. NAS, Romans 3:12.

29. NAS, Romans 3:11.

30. NAS, Luke 7:47.

31. NAS, John 1:14.

32. NAS, John 14:6.

33. NAS, John 17:17.

34. Chuck Colson, How Now Shall We Live, (Wheaton, Illinois: Tyndale House Publishers, Inc., 1999) p. 22.

35. Ibid., p. 23.

36. Allan Bloom, The Closing Of The American Mind, (New York: Harcourt Brace, 1963) p. 156.

37. Randy Alcorn, The Grace and Truth Paradox, (Sisters, OR: Multnomah Publishers, 2003) p. 58.

38. Alcorn, p. 56-57.

39. NAS, Isaiah 58:8-9.

40. NAS, Deut. 29:29.

41. NAS, John 8:32.

42. NAS, Proverbs 14:12.

43. Elizabeth Dodds, Marriage To A Difficult Man, (Laurel, MS: Audubon Press, 2004) (Original edition published by Westminster Press, 1971), p. 37-39.

44. Ibid, p. 39-41.

45. Michael Kruger, RTS Journal: A Postmodern Christmas, Winter 2002 p.4

46. NAS, 2 Corinthians 10:5.

47. NAS, John 8:32.

48. C.S. Lewis, The Lion, The Witch and The Wardrobe, (New York: Scholastic, 1995), p. 80.

49. Randy Alcorn, The Grace and Truth Paradox, (Multnomah Publishers, 2003) p. 21.

50. C.S. Lewis, The Voyage of The Dawn Treader, (New York: Collier Books, 1970), pp. 214-215.

51. Lewis, Mere Christianity,. (HarperSan Francisco Zondervan Publishing House, 2001) p. 52.

NOTES

NOTES

NOTES

_____

_____

_____

_____

_____

_____

_____

_____

_____

_____

_____

_____

_____

_____

_____

_____

_____

_____